Xia—

I heard that you have a very special Roo in your life. So I'm sure you already know: Roos are precious, loving souls, just like you!

Big hugs.

Kelly Ryne
2022

This Book Belongs To:

Xia 🖤🖤

Because I Love Kangaroos!

For all wildlife lovers & protectors
both present and future

A heartfelt thank you to Sara and Gary, the two most dedicated kangaroo
rescuers you'll ever meet. Their friendship has changed my life forever.

To my loving husband Paul, for always encouraging me to follow my dreams,
and holding my hand every step of the way.

www.redrabbitbooks.com.au
www.kellyryner.com

978-0-6455696-0-5 (hardcover)
978-0-6455696-1-2 (paperback)
978-0-6455696-2-9 (ebook)

Maxie Roo

IS JUST LIKE YOU!

Written &
Illustrated by
Kelly Ryner

Kelly Ryner
12.22

Maxie Roo is a kangaroo;

because he's young, a joey too.

Up on the hill overlooking a stream,

at Red Rabbit Farm, he sits and he dreams.

I watch him all day, and just before night;
to see him so happy is my heart's delight.

I watch and I ponder, might you also care?
I gave it some thought, and I felt I should share.

Though a kid kangaroo,

he's no different from you.

After playtime or sleep,

Max is ready to eat.

His nails are for digging;
eating dirt helps with gas
He loves picking flowers
and grabbing long grass.

He enjoys a good stretch
and a belly scratch too;
then comes a fart and
a really good poo.

He watches the birds, butterflies, and the bugs.
Curious Max — even tasted a slug!

Hard to believe, but really, it's true!
I saw it one morning; it made me say, "Ewww!"

Max always naps in the midst of the day;
he hides in the shade when it's too hot to play.
Resting's for thinking, so it isn't bad;
he readies for boxing with his dear old dad.

Max has a best friend;
her name is Indie.

They both feel so anxious when it gets too windy.

If the wind is too loud, it's a challenge to hear . . .

and so hard to know when danger is near.

They welcome the rain; it turns their world green.
Max enjoys puddles, but Indie stays clean.

Indie's more cautious, but she's not at all wrong;
together their differences make them both strong.

Max is so bold, Indie thinks that he's brave.

His mother might tell you that he misbehaves.

With speed and excitement, Max jumps up so high,

for no other reason than to make the birds fly.

One day to the bush Indie ran in great fear!

Max swiftly hopped after, but she disappeared.

She had spied a red fox; off quickly she raced…

'cause there's nothing as scary as being chased.

They got a bit lost, a bit turned around…

but were so relieved when each other they found.

The pair made a plan;
their steps they retraced,
Along past the creek they
hopped in great haste,
over a rock,
around the gum tree,
down in the pasture
they finally could see . . .

...a big group of roos, in the red setting sun,
eating and playing and just having fun.

His kangaroo mob has sisters and brothers,
but there's nothing as precious as the love of his mother.
She hugs him so tightly, his head to her chest.
Her cuddles and kisses are the absolute best.

I've said it before; I hope you now know it's true.

Though Maxie's a roo, he is just like you!

He wants to grow up; have kids of his own,

so we must protect — both him and his home.

How can you help?

- Never buy or eat any kangaroo products. With a simple online search, you will be surprised at what is sold around the world using kangaroo skin.

- Remind your parents to drive more carefully during early mornings and early evenings when kangaroos are more apt to be along roadways.

- If you see a kangaroo that is hurt, immediately call your local wildlife rescue organization.

- Join a group that can train you in animal care.

- Support wildlife conservation organizations.

Between bottle feeds and long walks in the bush, while raising orphaned Max and Indie, this book was born. They are distinctly different in their personalities and to know them is to love them. They have been a wonder to watch growing up and assimilating into our resident kangaroo mob enjoying their wildlife oasis that is Red Rabbit Farm in Cobargo, NSW Australia.

A minimum of 50% of all profits received by the writer/illustrator for this book will be distributed to local sanctuaries and veterinarians looking after kangaroo rescue & welfare.

Kelly Ryner

www.kellyryner.com

Printed in Australia
AUHW012209061122
371185AU00001B/1

9 780645 569605